SUSIE BROOKS

LET'S MAKE

ART

WITH

SCRAP PAPER

First published in Great Britain in 2016 by Wayland

ISBN: 978 0 7502 9825 4
10 9 8 7 6 5 4 3 2 1

Printed in China

Wayland
An imprint of
Hachette Children's Group
Part of Hodder and Stoughton
Carmelite House
50 Victoria Embankment
London EC4Y 0DZ

An Hachette UK Company
www.hachette.co.uk
www.hachettechildrens.co.uk

Editor: Elizabeth Brent
Design: nicandlou

CONTENTS

Flighty Kites p.26-27

Dangly Dragons p.10-11

People Pyramid p.24-25

Bright Bunch p.8-9

Birds in Boots p 14-15

LET'S MAKE ART!

HOW OFTEN DO YOU THROW OLD FOOD PACKAGING, WRAPPING PAPER OR LEAFLETS INTO THE RECYCLING? NEXT TIME YOU DO, STOP AND LOOK! SCRAP PAPER AND CARD IS PERFECT FOR MAKING ALL SORTS OF ARTWORK, AS YOU'LL FIND OUT IN THIS BOOK.

WHAT YOU NEED

If you like the colours on an old cereal packet, tissue box or magazine photo, save it! Even black-and-white newspaper can be turned into brilliant designs. You can use the back of old envelopes or cardboard boxes as the base for your pictures. Ribbons, cupcake cases and doilies are great for extra bits of decoration.

FOR THE PROJECTS IN THIS BOOK IT ALSO HELPS TO HAVE A FEW BASIC ART SUPPLIES:

- ✓ a pencil and rubber
- ✓ scissors
- ✓ glue
- ✓ plain white paper or card
- ✓ coloured paper or card, including black
- ✓ coloured pencils
- ✓ felt-tip pens
- ✓ crayons
- ✓ a ruler
- ✓ a hole punch
- ✓ double-sided sticky tape
- ✓ a sponge

HANDY HINTS

Before you start, lay down plenty of newspaper to protect the surface you're working on.

To pick up tiny bits of paper like the circles from a hole punch, lick your finger and the paper will cling to it.

Work at a size you feel comfortable with - if something's too fiddly to cut, try doing it bigger.

Save scraps of paper that you've cut away - they'll be useful another time!

Nail scissors are handy for cutting small paper shapes. Some craft scissors have a special zig-zag blade for fancy edges.

If you don't have paper in the colour you want, you can always paint your own.

When you see this LOGO, you might want to ask an adult to help.

There are templates on PAGES 30-31 to help you draw some useful shapes, but don't try to copy everything exactly. Half the fun is testing ideas of your own!

BATTY SILHOUETTES

USE COLOURED TISSUE PAPER PACKAGING TO MAKE THESE BATTY BACKGROUNDS.

1 Tear up scraps of tissue paper and glue them to a sheet of white paper or card. Keep going until the paper is covered. Don't worry if you only have one or two colours. You can overlap the pieces to create different shades.

2 When your paper is full, draw around a mug, glass or roll of sticky tape and cut out several circles.

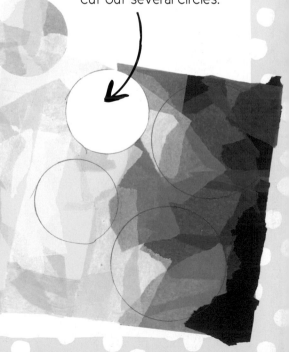

3 Now practise drawing bat shapes like this one. Make them small enough to fit inside your tissue paper circles. Copy them on to black paper and cut them out. There are some templates on p.30 to help you.

BRIGHT BUNCH

TRANSFORM OLD SCRAPS OF WRAPPING PAPER, WALLPAPER AND OTHER PATTERNED PAPER INTO A COLOURFUL VASE OF FLOWERS.

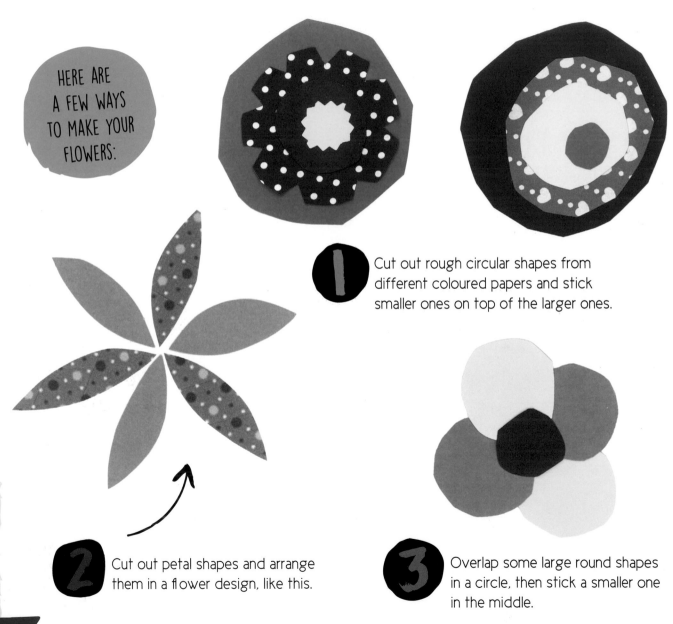

HERE ARE A FEW WAYS TO MAKE YOUR FLOWERS:

1 Cut out rough circular shapes from different coloured papers and stick smaller ones on top of the larger ones.

2 Cut out petal shapes and arrange them in a flower design, like this.

3 Overlap some large round shapes in a circle, then stick a smaller one in the middle.

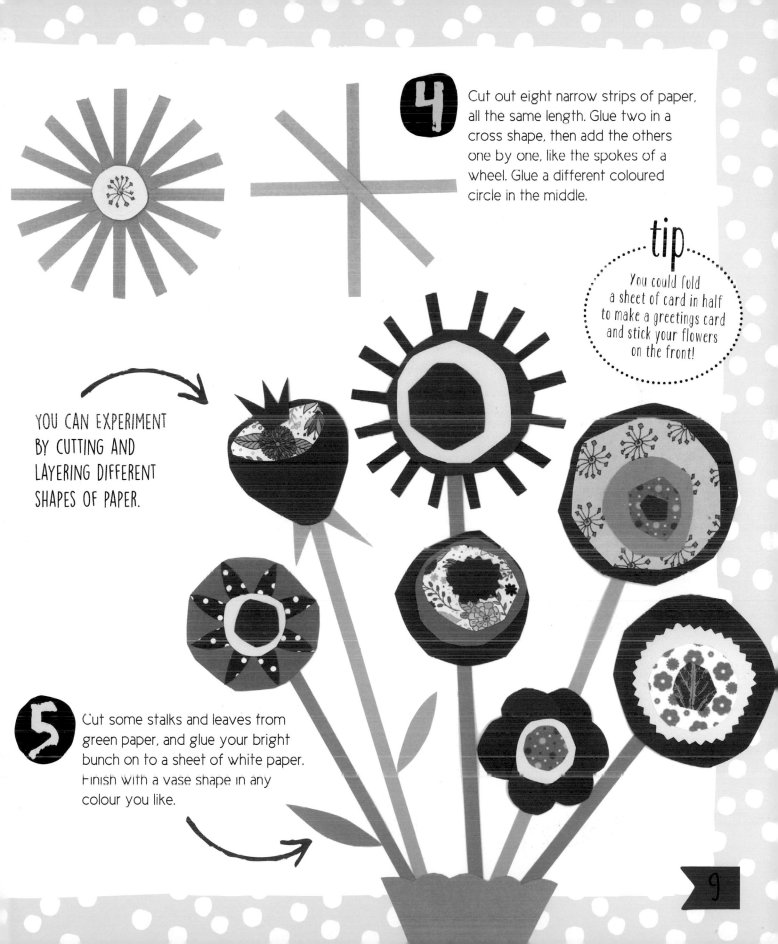

4 Cut out eight narrow strips of paper, all the same length. Glue two in a cross shape, then add the others one by one, like the spokes of a wheel. Glue a different coloured circle in the middle.

tip
You could fold a sheet of card in half to make a greetings card and stick your flowers on the front!

YOU CAN EXPERIMENT BY CUTTING AND LAYERING DIFFERENT SHAPES OF PAPER.

5 Cut some stalks and leaves from green paper, and glue your bright bunch on to a sheet of white paper. Finish with a vase shape in any colour you like.

DANGLY DRAGONS

USE SCRAPS OF COLOURED CARD OR PACKAGING TO MAKE THESE FRIENDLY FIRE-BREATHERS.

THESE LITTLE CIRCLES OF PAPER CAME OUT OF A HOLE PUNCH.

1 Cut out a triangle for the head, about 5 cm wide at the top. There's a template on p.30 if you need it.

2 Glue the triangle on to a piece of scrap paper, then stick on smaller shapes like these ones to create a face. Cut the whole thing out.

3 Cut out an arrow shape for the tail, and lots of narrow strips, 7 or 8 cm long, for the body. Make some straight and others wiggly or spiky.

4 Find a piece of ribbon or wool and lay it on a sheet of newspaper. Dot glue all along it. Stick the strips crossways, so the ribbon lies in the middle. Cut off any spare ribbon at the ends and glue the tail to one end and the head to the other.

YOU CAN DANGLE YOUR DRAGON BY ITS TAIL OR PIN IT TO A WALL OR PINBOARD.

SWIRLY SNAIL

WRAPPING PAPER AND WALLPAPER SCRAPS
WORK WELL FOR THIS SMILEY SNAIL.

1 Roughly cut out a circle from plain–coloured paper, about the size of a small plate or bowl. This will be the background for the snail's shell.

2 Using bits of patterned paper, cut out lots of pointy triangle shapes to fit in the circle, like this.

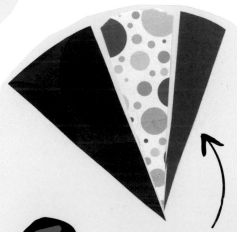

3 Arrange the triangles with the points in the middle of the circle, and glue them down.

A BLACK–AND–WHITE SNAIL
MADE FROM NEWSPAPER IS
FUN TO DO, TOO.

4 When your shell is complete, draw a snail's body on different coloured paper. The outline might look a bit like this – there's a template on p.31 that you can trace if you want.

ADD SOME EYES ON STALKS AND A MOUTH!

5 Cut out the snail's body and glue on the shell.

BIRDS IN BOOTS

CREATE A FLOCK OF BIRDS WEARING COLOURFUL WELLY BOOTS!

1 Practise drawing bird shapes like these, with a rounded head and a pointed tail. Draw some on to scrap paper and cut them out.

2 Glue your bird shapes on to white paper and draw around them. Cut out wing and beak shapes and stick them on. Draw two legs and an eye.

WHY NOT TRY MAKING A HEN, A DUCK OR A PARROT!

YOU COULD ADD SOME SWIRLY TAIL FEATHERS.

3 Cut out some boot shapes from spare wrapping paper or wallpaper, or paint your own patterns.

NOW DRESS UP YOUR BIRDS IN SOME BOOTS!

4 Glue the boots over the ends of your birds' legs.

THIS KITCHEN CLOTH MAKES A GREAT PUDDLE.

15

FRUIT TROOP

A FEW SIMPLE SHAPES CAN MAKE A PRETTY PATTERN!

1 You'll need a selection of paper squares, all the same size, in a few different colours. One way to make these is to cut strips 6 cm wide from a sheet of paper, then mark every 6 cm along the strip and cut into squares.

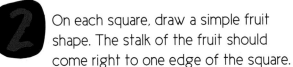

2 On each square, draw a simple fruit shape. The stalk of the fruit should come right to one edge of the square.

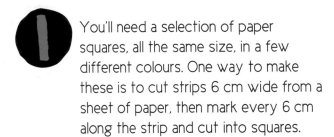

LEAVES CAN BE FIDDLY TO CUT, SO LEAVE THEM OUT IF YOU WANT TO MAKE IT EASIER.

3 Carefully cut all around the fruit, starting from the stalk. Keep both the inside and the outside piece whole. When you've cut out one piece of fruit, you can draw around it on a different coloured square!

4 Arrange your fruit shapes on a big sheet of dark-coloured paper. Put an outside piece next to an inside piece, and so on. Build up a colourful block. Try putting some pieces upside down or sideways.

WHEN YOU'RE HAPPY WITH YOUR DESIGN, GLUE THE PIECES DOWN. YOU COULD DISPLAY THE PICTURE IN YOUR KITCHEN.

NOSY BOOKMARKS

CARDBOARD ENVELOPES MAKE A GREAT BASE FOR THESE NOSY ANIMALS. SLOT THEM OVER A PAGE IN YOUR BOOK, WITH THE NOSE PEERING DOWN TO MARK YOUR PLACE.

1 Think of an animal with a long nose or snout, and draw the outline of its head on to card.

AN ELEPHANT MIGHT LOOK LIKE THIS!

RECTANGLE

SMALL ARCH

2 Cut out the head shape, then cut a rectangle for the body with a small arch between the legs, like this.

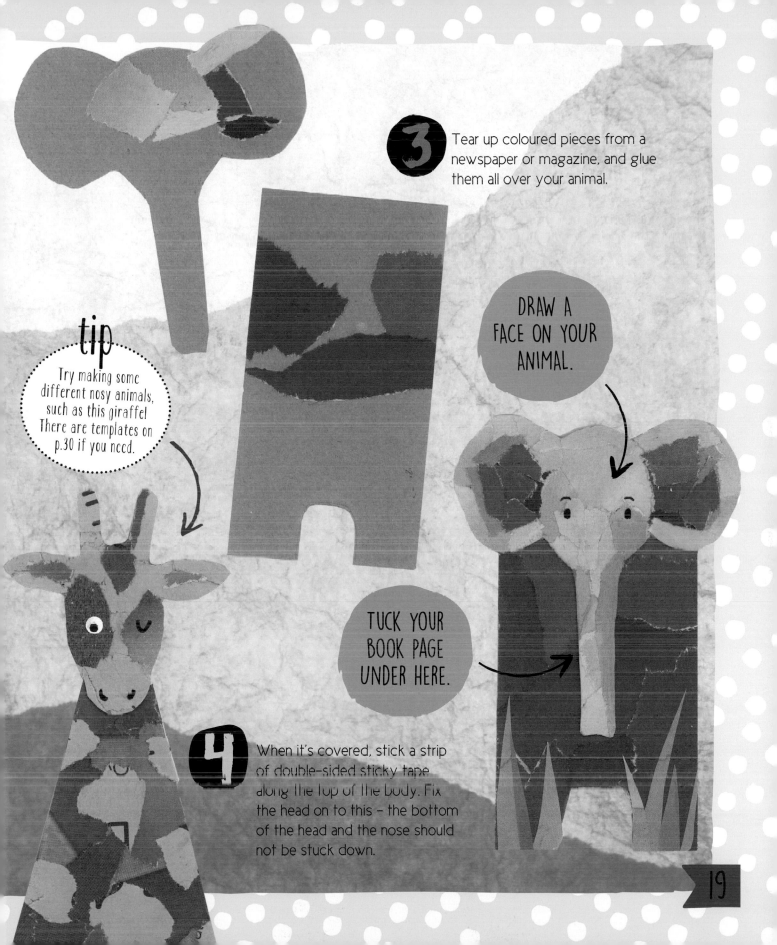

3 Tear up coloured pieces from a newspaper or magazine, and glue them all over your animal.

DRAW A FACE ON YOUR ANIMAL.

tip
Try making some different nosy animals, such as this giraffe! There are templates on p.30 if you need.

TUCK YOUR BOOK PAGE UNDER HERE.

4 When it's covered, stick a strip of double-sided sticky tape along the top of the body. Fix the head on to this – the bottom of the head and the nose should not be stuck down.

SHADY TREES

YOU DON'T NEED BRIGHTLY COLOURED PAPER TO CREATE AN EYE-CATCHING PICTURE!

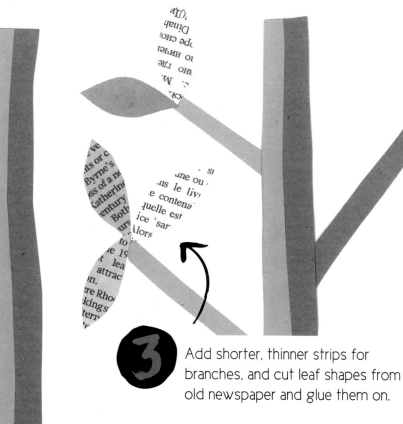

1 Cut a strip of brown parcel paper. Make the edges a bit wobbly, like a tree trunk. Glue it on to a white background.

3 Add shorter, thinner strips for branches, and cut leaf shapes from old newspaper and glue them on.

2 Now cut a narrower strip from a light brown envelope, the same height as your tree trunk. Stick this down one side of the trunk, to give the effect of light shining on it.

TRY CUTTING OUT OR DRAWING SOME ANIMALS TO HIDE AMONG YOUR TREES. THE DARK COLOURS HERE WERE CUT OUT FROM OLD MAGAZINES.

tip

If you make a tree the whole height of your paper, it will seem closer than the others.

4 You can create a shadow on the ground by cutting a strip of brown paper the width of the tree trunk and gluing it at an angle at the bottom of your tree trunk.

PUPS IN PRINT

SIMPLE TORN—UP NEWSPAPER IS PERFECT FOR THESE PUPS.

1 Tear a big oblong shape for the body and a smaller one for the head. Glue them to some plain paper.

MAKE YOUR DOG A BASKET OR A BONE.

2 Draw on legs, a tail, ears and a face, like these.

3 To make a shaggy dog, draw an outline of the animal in pencil – there are some templates on p.31 to help. Then tear up lots of thin strips of newspaper. Glue the top of each strip to the top of the dog and let the rest hang down.

USE STRIPS OF COLOURED NEWSPAPER FOR A BOW . . .

CUT OUT CLOUD SHAPES FOR A FLUFFY POODLE.

. . . OR A COLLAR!

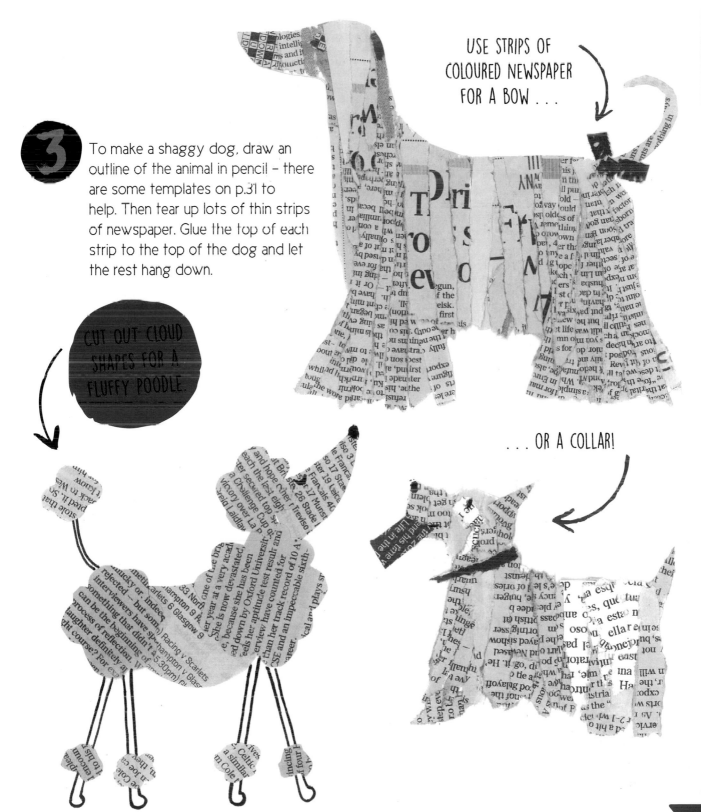

PEOPLE PYRAMID

YOU CAN HAVE LOTS OF FUN WITH SIMPLE COLLAGE FIGURES. GLUE THEM ON TO A PIECE OF WHITE PAPER OR CARD.

1 Cut out some head shapes from scrap paper or magazines. Draw or glue on different faces. Try using lips or ears from a photo! Punch some holes in paper with a hole punch, and use the little circles for eyes or cheeks.

2 Look for patterned paper and try cutting these simple shapes for clothes. You might find fabric textures in a catalogue. Cut strips for arms and legs, and two oval feet.

CUT OUT HAIR FROM PHOTOS!

3 When you've practised making people, try piling some up in a pyramid shape! Start with the bottom row, then perch the others on top.

CUT UP A PAPER DOILY FOR FRILLY CLOTHES.

YOU COULD ADD SOME PARTY HATS AND BOWS. THIS TUTU IS MADE FROM A CUPCAKE CASE!

25

FLIGHTY KITES

MIX AND MATCH DIFFERENT PAPERS FOR A FLURRY OF KITES FLYING HIGH!

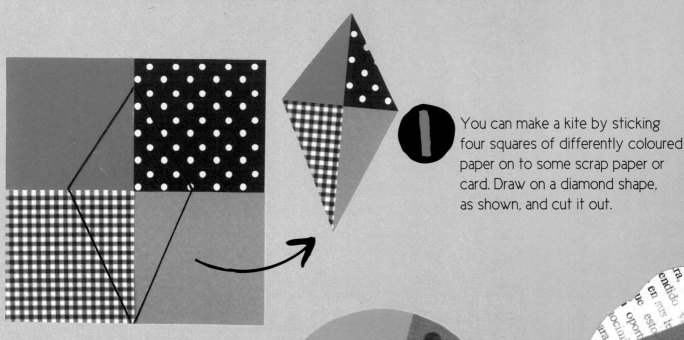

1 You can make a kite by sticking four squares of differently coloured paper on to some scrap paper or card. Draw on a diamond shape, as shown, and cut it out.

2 For a round kite, cut out two circles of the same size. Fold one of them in half, then into quarters, and cut along the folds. Glue two of the quarters on to the other whole circle from different coloured papers.

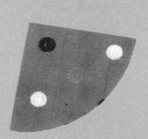

FOR THIS KITE, ARRANGE TRIANGLES IN A CIRCLE WITH THEIR NARROWEST POINT IN THE MIDDLE.

CUT OUT CLOUD SHAPES FROM
OLD NEWSPAPER AND SCRIBBLE
OVER THEM WITH WHITE
CRAYON OR PAINT.

ADD SOME COLOURFUL FLOWING
TAILS TO YOUR KITES USING STRIPS
OR TRIANGLES OF PAPER.

3 Glue everything on to a
piece of pale blue card.

WOVEN WALLS

WEAVE WINDOWS INTO SOME PAPERY CITY WALLS!

1 Fold a rectangle of paper – about half the width of a piece of A4 – in half, lengthways. Mark lines across from the folded edge, spacing them about 3 cm apart. Stop each line about a centimetre from the opposite edge. Cut along the lines and open the paper out.

3 CM

◀1 CM▶

WEAVE THESE IN AND OUT THROUGH THE SLITS.

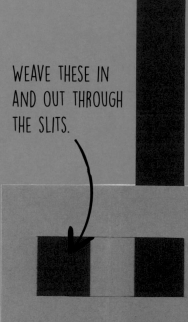

2 From a different coloured paper, cut out some strips the same height as your rectangle and about 2 cm wide.

TEMPLATES

BATS
P.6—7

DRAGON'S
FACE
P.10—11

ZEBRA AND
GIRAFFE
P.18—19

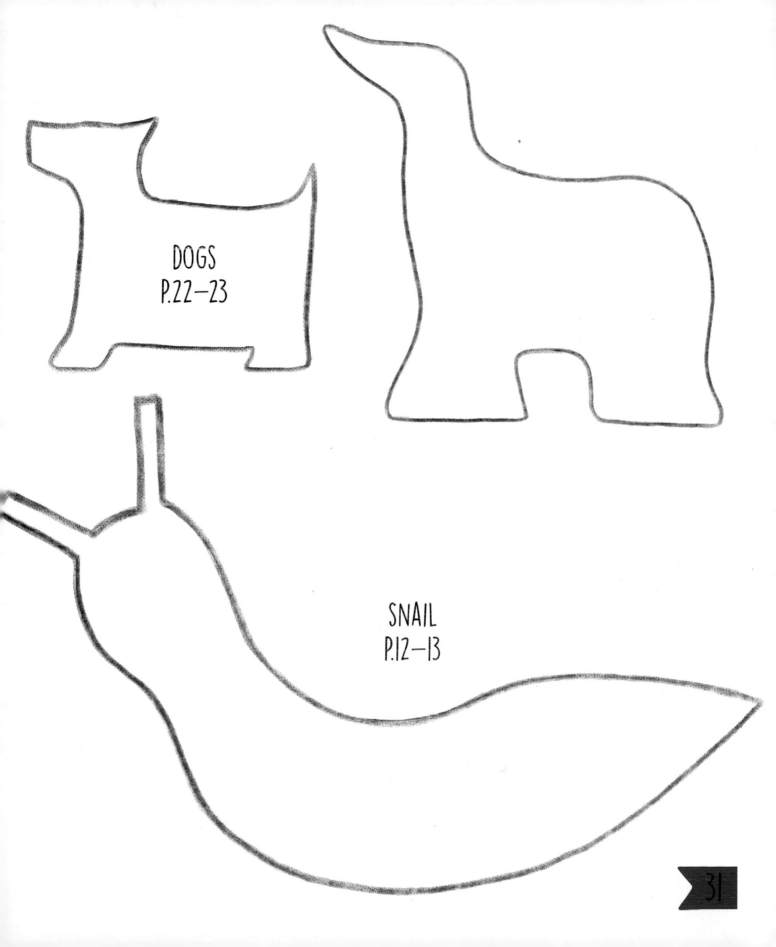

DOGS
P.22—23

SNAIL
P.12—13

GLOSSARY

COLLAGE art made by sticking bits of paper, fabric or other materials on to a surface

CORRUGATED ridged, like the inside layer of some cardboard

LAYERING arranging pieces on top of one another

OVERLAP to partly cover one shape with another

SILHOUETTE a plain dark shape, usually shown against a light or coloured background

WEAVE to combine threads or strips of paper at right angles to one another, by passing them over and under

TEMPLATE a shape used as a guideline to draw or cut around

TEXTURE the feel or appearance of a surface, such as fluffy wool

SUSIE BROOKS

LET'S MAKE ART WITH

SCRAP PAPER

9780750298254

SUSIE BROOKS

LET'S MAKE ART WITH

HANDS AND FEET

9781526300416

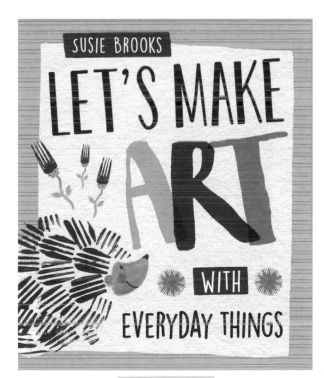

SUSIE BROOKS

LET'S MAKE ART WITH

EVERYDAY THINGS

9781526300447

SUSIE BROOKS

LET'S MAKE ART BY

PRINTING & STAMPING

9781526300454